Finish What You Start!

To:

From:

Date:

#ALLDONE

#ALLDONE

A R.E.A.L Practical Guide to
Go from College Student to
College Graduate

Dr. Zakia Robbins

Dr. Zakia Robbins

ISBN: 0-992142-0-9

ISBN-13: 978-0-9992142-0-6

Praise for #ALLDONE

"In just one hour it helped me make sense of numerous scattered ideas that I had been trying to organize for months. I still use the graph to this day!"

— Terrell Brown, *ImSoPhit*

"#ALLDONE guides the reader through challenges in getting what you want to get done, DONE!"

—Tien Sydnor-Campbell, *BodyMind Counseling & Consulting*

"I often find that I get overwhelmed by everything I have on my plate to get done because I am focused on *the forest* and not *the trees*. #ALLDONE assisted with organizing those trees so the tasks got done instead of sitting in a never-ending queue. Sometimes I did not understand the process but, with the tips found in the book, I definitely trust the process because I ended up in a better place at the end."

—Tai Harris, *HOM Group LLC*

"This book will show you how to get to the top of the mountain so you can yell #ALLDONE!!!"

— Bianca Lewis, *Event Curator*

"As a busy mom, corporate America employee and healthy lifestyle coach for women, I have found these tips to be a god-send! You learn how to go from overwhelmed to accomplished QUICKLY by learning very relatable and actionable steps."

— Joyce N. Robinson, *Redesign U*

"Each time that I get in a tough spot, I use the strategies and skills to help me not only to get out of that spot, but also those to prevent them from occurring again. This is such an invaluable resource."

— Dr. Quornelia Hypolite, *Educator*

"These practical sense and task oriented methods helped me immensely. This is a much needed book!"

— A. Sutton-Bey, *Professional Development Coach*

"Wow! As a mother working full-time and going to school full-time, I found myself asking all the questions answered in the book!

— Jerelyn Tolbert, *JToneBody Fitness*

Behind
The Book

8 chapters

As you read this book, you will notice that there are 8 chapters. There is much significance in the number 8. According to Doreen Virtue, of Angel Therapy, the "number 8 represents infinity and everything good in the universe which is infinite such as infinite love, infinite supply, infinite energy, infinite time... 8 represents complete and unending abundance without any lack." The main significance of the number 8 is the fact that I am using it to pay homage to my family. I am the oldest of 8 children. My mother raised all 8 of us, as a single parent, in one home. This book is for my mother and brothers.

What I learned from...

Throughout this book, I will drop some names, podcasts and books that I found out about and used along my journey. By all means, check these out too! What I value and what you value will surely be different. Go ahead and look, listen and preview for yourself!

Setting the tone

I'd like to start off by setting the tone of this guide. While you're in school, you could use one less textbook to read, therefore, I'd like you to look at this like a coffee-table read. Imagine that you are at your favorite coffee shop having a conversation with a friend. Yup, I'm your friend. Your friend that's here to help you get and stay on track. We will have a conversation about the pitfalls you might experience while working hard and going to school. We will also talk about some strategies and techniques you can use along the process. You'll hear some short (very short) stories about people who have used the techniques you'll read about later. Well, that's it for now, now let's get started...

#ALLDONE

Contents

Chapter 1

Mission: Q & A

1: Mission: Q&A

Vignette

As I stand here in my favorite coffee shop, I can't help but be humbled by the fact that I am writing a book about success strategies for college students and adult learners. Right before I started writing this afternoon, I realized that I needed to complete a few school assignments of my own before I could start the process of helping you… after all, how can I help you when I don't get my own tasks/assignments out of the way first, right? Anyway, my assignment is done and submitted, so now, I can focus on you. Helping you succeed is my ultimate passion, so hopefully, you will find value in what I'm presenting to you.

For the sake of discussion, let's begin by looking at everything I have chosen to take on at this time in my life, I'm working on: attaining my 4th college degree, Master of Science in Curriculum and Instruction, full-time faculty at a technical college, online adjunct faculty with 2 active courses currently running and I'm also a behavioral specialist. I must also mention the fact that I'm also working on improving my physical and financial situation, so therefore, these things take time as well. Oh yea, I also like to socialize, so add that in too… I mention all of this to show you that it is possible to have a life outside of school while you're working to attain your degree. I'm here to show you how.

How can you live and complete your degree?

Live your life AND complete your degree. It is possible! I promise it is. Will you have to rearrange a few things in your life to be successful? Yup, you will, however, making some sacrifices will help make this all possible. Keep in the things that you absolutely must do, remove the things that don't help you get to your goal. It's easier said than done, however, I will walk you through numerous activities to help you through this process. I want you to have fun while you work towards your degree, because after all, all work and no play is just plain boring. Balance is key. Balance is necessary.

You have so many barriers, how can you even start?

This morning during my 3-mile run, I was listening to one of my favorite podcasts, "The Model Health Show with Shawn Stevenson." In this episode titled, "The 4 Barriers To Break Through When Building Your Body and Your Life," he and his co-host discussed some common barriers that they hear when people are looking to change any aspect of their life. When discussing barriers, he hit the nail on the head with this, "there's always a way over them, under them, around them or even straight through them." I stopped running at this point because I needed to process what I heard. I thought to myself, how many times have you allowed your barriers to be the answer to your question? How many times have you said " I want to do _____, but I can't because of _____?" The light switch in my head immediately turned on. We get in our own way and then wonder what happened to our goals and dreams years down the road.

Let's just get this out of the way right now: you are not the first person ever in life to have barriers while you work to earn your degree. In preparation for this book, I spoke to many people who also experienced barriers in their life, more specifically, while they were working to earn a degree or certificate. Yes, you need to work, take care of your family or do other things while you are going back for your degree. I get it, believe me I do. But, let me say it again and just to make it stick out, I'm going to say it like this: YOU ARE NOT THE FIRST PERSON EVER IN LIFE TO HAVE BARRIERS WHILE YOU WORK TO EARN YOUR DEGREE. Ok, now that we got one of the most common excuses out of the way, we can move on. EVERYONE you meet has barriers, however, how we decide to let those barriers impact us is what ultimately matters.

What methods exist for helping college students get organized?

As I started to write this book, I looked around for the best productivity and time management books, articles, podcasts, apps, etc. I could find. David Allen is the guru of this discussion. In his book "Getting Things Done," you can find a lot of tips, techniques, etc. to help you be more efficient during the day. As I read the book and listened to his podcasts, I was surprised that he actually had names for some of the things I already do. Things such as creating a list, identifying goals and maintaining tidy spaces where you work are mentioned in his work which I already implement myself. His work is GENIUS!

While Allens' work, and many other time management specialists cover the time management aspect, I haven't found anything or anyone in the time management area that is speaking directly to college students and adult learners about this subject. Yes, there are study guides out there, however, these also do not talk about how to accomplish the goal of finishing school while having a life outside of school. In the time management and productivity area, the message is pretty clear: organize and list what you need to do, then take the steps to get it done. In terms of earning a college degree, the message is pretty clear as well: do your schoolwork, pass your courses and you'll earn your degree. While I agree with both ideas, I wondered why no one ever thought to combine the two ideas together in a practical manner.

In this book, I will be reviewing strategies that combine traditional time management and productivity strategies, along with what I know to be true about behaviors needed to be a successful college student or adult learner. In combining these concepts, the idea is that you will find strategies that work for you and your situation. I can tell you what worked for me, however, you finding what works for you and successfully attaining your degree is my primary objective.

You have so much going on, where do you even start?

Whether you are about to start school, you are currently in school or you are almost finished school, this book is for you. If you are anything like me, I want to be as efficient as possible. Whenever I get new information, I try to apply it as soon as I can, especially if it will help ease stress, anxiety and confusion. While working on my current degree, my 4th college degree if you've been paying attention, I realized that I already had a system to accomplish my tasks both in and out of the classroom, however, it started to fail me. I needed to do something else, and I needed to do it quick.

There was something about working on this current degree that caused me to be stressed and overwhelmed a lot. I don't know if it was because I was traveling so much (on top of what I was already doing), trying to find my life's purpose, or questioning where my life was at the time, but I REALLY felt like I was burning the candle at both ends. Truth be told, I was so overwhelmed that I could not do anything. I mean like, stay in and do absolutely nothing type of overwhelmed. By the time I snapped out of this funk (funks because it started to happen more frequently than I could remember), I had to do a lot of tasks, with less time to meet the deadlines. I don't know if you are like me, but I had no choice but to develop these strategies, because otherwise, I would be all over the place without a plan. If I remained in that state, I would've collapsed and burned, literally and figuratively.

There's so much information out there, how do you know what will or won't work for you?

I agree, there is so much information on productivity and time management that it can be downright overwhelming! I have researched countless methods in my quest to find the best things that have worked for me or those people that I have helped along the way. As I come upon these strategies, I will point out where I learned it, so you can take a look as well. As you read through these pages, I hope that you find strategies that work for you. Even if what you read lights a spark for you to do some more research to find additional strategies, I'll still feel like I met my goal for you.

I have taken the time to review some of the best strategies I have found along my journey. While I believe that I have done some of the work for you, I know that this is not a fully exhaustive compilation of what's out there. During this journey, I found a guy named Chris Bailey, who did a year worth of research about the subject. In his book titled, "The Productivity Project," Chris tried everything there is to try regarding productivity. This is worth a mention because yes, I learned a lot from him. To me, why recreate the wheel, he did the research so we wouldn't have to. I've pulled a few things from him as well as others to present to you. Take what works, leave what doesn't.

How do you know you're doing it right?

If it works, you'll know. Just like if it doesn't, you'll know that too. It should be almost effortless. It will turn into a way of life. It will become automatic. You might not be able to get through your day without it. When any or all of these happen, then, you'll know. Just like a kid learning to walk, you'll experience some bumps along the way. Hopefully these bumps don't make you quit, however, I would be lying if I didn't say that you will have some growing pains. This happens to all of us learning new things. Understand this and embrace it as well. This will get you very far, in this book and in life. It will just feel right. Plain and simple.

How can these rituals and habits help you attain your degree?

The discussion about habits and rituals was something that I picked up from a podcast titled, "The Productivity Show," by Asian Efficiency. The general premise of their podcast is to "learn everything about time management, life hacks and productivity." The co-hosts discuss rituals and habits across multiple podcasts, however, I found value in episode 84. During this episode they discussed everything from working out, efficiency systems and using pen and paper systems, amongst other life hacks.

According to Asian Efficiency, the habits and rituals become a way of life. For as long as you are working on your degree, you will need to develop rituals and habits to help keep you focused on the tasks at hand. The definition of a habit, per the Merriam-Webster dictionary is: a settled tendency or usual manner of behavior. Another definition used is: a behavior pattern acquired by frequent repetition. Merriam-Webster also define a ritual as: done in accordance with a social custom or normal protocol. Whether you are dealing with work, kids, play or school, you will need to have some sort of plan to navigate through life as you try to accomplish everything you have decided to take on. Identifying your habits and rituals will help you solidify your plan.

Chapter 2

Why We're Here

2: Why We're Here

Vignette

My quest for being more organized occurred out of sheer necessity. I have been diagnosed with chronic insomnia. For more than 30 years, I have not been able to get a restful sleep. I can probably write a book about that too, but I digress. Here's the deal, my chronic insomnia forced me to have to be efficient. You would think that if a person couldn't sleep, they might as well use the time to be productive, right? Well, I'm sorry to say, that did not work for me. I could not be productive in the middle of the night when I couldn't sleep, instead, it was more akin to being in fog. In addition to this, when you can't sleep at night, this also means that you are tired all day. The cycle of sleepless nights, tired all darn day was (and still is) my life. I had to find a way to make things happen, regardless of whether or not I was tired all day. This system I present to you later in this book, continues to help me succeed in school and in life. Sleep, or lack thereof, cannot, and will not, be my downfall!

I'm here to help

Who better to help you than someone who has already done it many times over? A little history about me, I do not come from parents who went to college, however, I knew I wanted to go to college and further my education. I had to rely on my village, community and network of people I did have around me for support with this aspect of my life. I remember my cousin coming home from college and me being in awe of her college stories, not just the stories about fun but I digress.

I'm sitting here writing to you, however, this is helping me identify where my drive to be a successful college student and adult learner came from. I was not forced to go to college. My mother was happy with me graduating from high school without making her a grandmother. The bar was set pretty low for me. While my experience is different than yours, the idea is still the same: look to those that have already done what you are trying to do. Use the information that works, do not use the information that does not work.

My experience

I'm going to show you what I learned along my 10+ year journey as a college student and adult learner. While this book will not give you everything there is to know about the subject, this is a great start. I have a Bachelor of Fine Arts, Master of Science, a Doctor of Management, and am currently working on a Master of Science in Curriculum and Instruction. Each degree I have earned is working together perfectly to help me meet my personal goals, and now, I sit here before you. I have implemented these strategies each time I decided to work towards a degree or training program, and now, I am finally systematizing these strategies for mass consumption.

Houston White, CEO of Houston White Men's Room (HWMR) and Black Excellence, the brand, and I had a candid conversation about how he garnered information from others. When asked about how he learned so many trades which included being a barber, building houses and now building his Black Excellence brand, he stated "that was my strategy to learn, I learned what I needed to know and I applied it immediately. Find somebody who is doing it or has done it and latch onto them." There truly is no better way to learn than to learn from someone else who has already successfully done what you are now trying to do.

The college classroom and beyond

For those of you that just want the degree to get the paper and move on with your life, I don't know what to tell you, but I'll try. If the degree in your hand is your motivation, use it to the best of your ability. If you want to be the first person in your family with a degree, use that to the best of your ability. If you absolutely, positively, love learning, then by all means, use this to your advantage. It does not matter what your motivation is, use it to your benefit. Focus on that! Day in and day out, focus on your motivation. Robert Farris, Chairman and President of the CoNimby Foundation, made a similar comment, "create a plan and do what you need to succeed. When times get rough, focus on your motivation. When something happens to make you lose focus, shift your focus right back to your motivation." You can do this! This is what successful people do. You're here because you too, want to be successful!

In most fields, after you complete your degree, you will be required to complete some sort of continuing education. Even if you decide that a degree is not for you, maybe you only take courses and get certifications that are specific to what you do now for work. In a conversation with Jay Connor, Writer/Founder and Co-Host of "The Extraordinary Negroes," he discussed how he absolutely did everything he could do to avoid school, however, when it came to taking practical courses that he could use in his field, he was all for it. If he wanted to learn how to be screenwriter, he took courses to make him better. This is all one and the same. What you learn in this book can be applied to any training, certificate or other type of educational setting. You will simply do what you learn here, time and time again.

Improve focus

In this book, you will find ways to improve your ability to focus on what you need to accomplish. I will provide you with strategies that have worked for me in the past and continue to work for me today. Additionally, I have worked with others who have had similar success. Simply put, you can focus on whatever you want to focus on. This book will help you identify rituals and habits you can adopt into your daily life. I will say this repeatedly: use what you can, disregard what you cannot.

Obstacles

Let's discuss obstacles, because after all, this is one of the reasons why you are here, right? Everyone has obstacles to endure throughout their life. Yes, yours might be different than mine and the next persons, however, obstacles are obstacles. Here's a deep thought that I want you to remember: as long as there is breath in your body, you are capable of overcoming your obstacles! Hold onto that! Bury it deep within your memory bank.

As I sit here writing, I think about the numerous obstacles I had to face while working to earn my degrees. I also think about the obstacles my peers faced while earning their degrees. Yes, some people did not make it. Statistically, I was not supposed to make it! Yet, I feel like I have and I still am not done. I would love to see you add your name to the list of people that earned their degree(s), despite the obstacles and challenges they had to face.

I'll show you how, you must do the work

While I cannot sit with you as you do your schoolwork or go through life, I can provide you with tools that you can use to be successful. Life will get stressful and things will happen throughout the course of your time in school, however, you can still succeed at earning your degree. What I am giving you are some tools, but you, my friend, must do the work.

In a discussion with Leonard Edwards, Senior Director of corporate partnerships of the New Jersey Devils and Team Dignitas, he discussed how you must be willing to hustle and grind to get to your goal. You must be willing to do the work. You must be willing to go above and beyond to attain your goals, because after all, these are your goals. You will create a name for yourself. The work you put in will definitely show. Be willing to do the work.

The plan

In theory, a plan is a roadmap that you use to get from where you are to where you want to be. As the reader of this book, I'm sure you've come up with plans for yourself in the past. Financial plans, fitness plans, success plans, etc. Plans help you see when you're on course or when you've gotten off course, therefore, it's important that you have a plan for whatever it is you'd like to accomplish. In the next chapter, I will discuss my R.E.A.L. simple plan for getting your degree and managing your life in the process. While I understand task organization and time management is not simple for everyone, I hope that by the end of this book, you will see that it really is a simple process that you can use every day.

Chapter 3

R.E.A.L.
Simple

3: R.E.A.L. Simple

Joyce and DaVita

Joyce and DaVita are the Co-Founders of #DreamsGoalsVision. Using a vision board party format, Joyce and DaVita walk you through a series of questions and activities to help you identify your goals and vision. While working with other participants, you use photos, quotes and words cut out from magazines with the hopes of creating a vision board that you will hang up in a place that you'll see every day. The premise behind vision boards is that if you see it daily, the vision will remain strong and everything you do daily will help get you closer to that goal.

I was called in to help Joyce and DaVita organize their business calendars, lives and everything in between, in a simple fashion. Let me tell you something real quick about these ladies: both are hard-working mothers, both have at least one other business aside from #DreamGoalsVision, both have lives outside of their children and both are just straight badasses (can I say that?). Anyway, I recall showing them my plan and thinking it was so simple, I thought everyone knew how to do this. The shock on their faces as well as them pointing out what I taught them, helped me solidify what I now coin my REAL simple approach.

The approach

The R.E.A.L simple approach was coined shortly after I sat with the 2 ladies mentioned in the vignette. What was simple and easy to me, was foreign in principle to them. I recall when I left the session with them thinking to myself: there are only 24 hours in a day, you have to identify what is important and do that. I also left thinking, there a lot of folks that have a lot to do, I wonder if they think about what they can accomplish in the span of 24 hours. This approach, focuses on these principles. In short, you focus on only what needs to get done, not what doesn't. You also learn to account for everything that takes up time: driving, waiting, preparation, etc. You must account for these things as you are creating your daily plans. I'll show you how a little later.

R: Realistic

You must be realistic. By realistic, I mean, you must have a plan in place that makes sense. Let's think about this in terms of courses, just to keep on topic. You start school and of course you want to graduate, right? The best option is to take all of your courses for your degree in one semester, right? Totally makes sense! NOT!!! Unless you are in a certificate or training program, this will not work. You have to lay out your courses in a realistic manner. You also have to remember that you want to have a life outside of school as well, right? So please be realistic about what you are trying to accomplish.

- ☐ **Action item #1: Fill in the blank: To earn my degree, I will take _____ courses per semester. This will allow me take care of _____, _____ and _____ outside of school.**

E: Easy

Whatever method(s) you decide to go with, make it easy. You have enough to deal with, overcomplicating things only makes things worse. The easier, the better. In all seriousness, the method should be easy because it increases the chances of you implementing it into your daily life, and using the method for life.

- ☐ **Action item #2: Review the statement and sign: I commit to creating an easy method for myself. Signed**

  _____

A: Attainable

To attain your goal, you must schedule your day so that you can ATTAIN almost everything on your list. Have you ever looked at someone's task list and it had 1,000,000 items on it for the day? I have! Impossible, right? Yes, I'm being sarcastic, however, I had to say it to get my point across. I know that adding too many tasks to your list for the day is the best way to overwhelm yourself. As you go through planning your day, make sure that you are only adding things that must and can be handled on that specific day.

☐ **Action item #3: Review the statement and sign: I will only add items to the day, that I know I will have time to work on. Signed _____**

L: Livable

This is a livable, breathable process and plan. It can be enjoyable. Now, I love lists and organization. I love lists, organization AND marking my listed tasks off as complete. It took me a while to solidify a process that worked for me. The same will happen to you. Feel free to play around with the different options and amend/update accordingly. This is by you and for you. Make it work for you and your life.

☐ **Action item #4: Review the statement and sign: I commit to making this a livable process. This process is for me and by me. I will make it work for me and my life. Signed _____**

Take your time

Just like a baby learning to walk, nailing down a process that works for you will take some time. Give yourself time to figure out what works for you and your situation. As you go through your courses, start to use some of the strategies listed in this book. As you progress through your courses, you will find your natural rhythm to how you successfully get things done, both in and out of the classroom. This process does not have to be torture. It can actually be quite fun! Don't be hard on yourself. You are taking on a lot of things and with a plan, you will succeed.

You can do this!

You can do this! You are in your training or degree program and ready to commit to getting it done. Yes, you have things to do outside of school, and that's ok. You will succeed! Why? Because you said so. You will give it your all. You will give it all you've got! There are people that believe in you, I am one of them!

Chapter 4

Before You Begin

4: Before You Begin

Shenise

Shenise is a single-mother with 2 kids. She has a multitude of degrees which include an MSS, MBA and she is currently practicing as a licensed clinical social worker. Shenise consults with a few behavioral and foster care agencies around the city in multiple capacities. Additionally, Shenise is a certified yoga instructor who loves to run. She is active in her church and can always be found helping others in need. This short synopsis merely cracks the surface of everything she does, however, for the sake of time and space, I kept her introduction concise.

I had the pleasure of sitting with Shenise as she was attempting to organize her life and all things in it. I walked Shenise through the activity that I am about to walk you through. As we sat across from one another at a coffee shop, I asked Shenise to pull out a sheet of paper and write out everything that she currently had to do on her agenda, which was currently all in her head (jobs, work out, church, etc). As she walked through this process, Shenise began to see just how much she does during the week. As she wrote things down on the paper, she recalled "oh, I also need to this," then she would think she was finished, only to yell out again, "oh, I do this too." It was fascinating to sit and listen as Shenise wrote out 1 page, front and back, of everything that she does. Just as she handed me the paper, I asked her, soooo, what about your kids? At this moment, we enjoyed a HEALTHY dose of laughter...

Your behavior dictates how far you will go

You did it! You're a college student or enrolled as an adult learner in a professional development program! You filled out applications, completed the requirements to get in, and now, here you are, ready to take classes. You did what you needed to do to get accepted into school, now the real work begins. Whether you believe it or not, by getting to this very point, you demonstrated that you have what it takes to succeed. You went through a step-by-step process to get into school, now, you must use very similar behavior and habits to complete your degree.

Your behavior dictates how far you will go in this process. Some people start, yet do not finish. I'm pretty sure that if you're reading this book, you want to be successful and earn your degree. Your behavior, while going through your courses, needs to be behavior like those of successful people. What have you set your sights on and successfully completed? Remember those behaviors you exhibited? Think about these for real! You must pull from that place again as you complete assignment after assignment, course after course. I'm not saying that it will be easy, but I am saying that it will be worth it.

Mindset

Having the right mindset will get you far, likewise, without the right mindset, you won't get anywhere. I like to think about mindset as being like the gas in your car. A car can't go very far without gas in the tank. Your mindset is very similar. Henry Ford once said, "whether you believe you can or can't, you're right." You must believe that you can do this, because you can! Speak what you seek only. Say it now, I WILL BE SUCCESSFUL! I WILL GET MY DEGREE!

As you go through your program, you will notice that you might lose steam. Believe me, it happens to ALL of us at one point or another. You will get tired. At times, you will feel defeated. I can honestly say that I have had these feelings myself, more than a few times. Heck, more times than I can count. For this latest degree, I've said to myself, "what the heck were you thinking?" I can smile when I say that now. I'm 2 classes away from getting my 4th college degree. Anything is possible, when you put your mind to it.

Don't know how to change your mindset? Focus on the possibilities. Think about what earning your degree will do for you. How will you feel when you earn your degree? See yourself walking across the stage at graduation or hanging your degree on the wall. If that doesn't work, find pictures, memes or quotes about success. If that doesn't work, find a podcast, video, song or another type of media to watch or listen to. I personally have done each and every one of these things, because believe me, there were times when I felt defeated. YouTube videos and podcasts helped me get back on track. I say, to each his/her own. Do what works for you, but the goal is getting your mindset on point. Find what works and do that.

Value

Only do things that add value. Ever been pulled in so many directions that you don't know where to start? Ever have the feeling that you need to go to everything you are invited to; however, you're only going or doing it because you kinda feel like you have to? Yup, me too. I'm going to let you in on a BIG secret: only do things that add value to your life. I'm going to say it again just in case you missed it: ONLY DO THINGS THAT ADD VALUE TO YOUR LIFE. I learned this from two guys that call themselves "The Minimalists." In their documentary *minimalism*, a documentary about the important things, podcast and book about the same topic, they discuss the idea that you should only do things that add value. From experience, I can tell you that this practice alone helped keep me focused, not just on school related activities, but in life in general.

"How do I apply this to my life," you ask? Well, I can help you with that. Let's start with thinking about the last time you said "yes" to something that you really wanted to say "no" to. How much time did you spend engaging in that activity? If you had to drive to and from the activity, add that time in there too. Did you shower and get dressed for this activity? Yup, add that in too. How much time did you spend engaging in an activity that you didn't want to do in the first place? Ok, now think about what else you could've done with that time. Something that added value perhaps. Could you have completed an assignment in that timeframe? Did you chuckle after that activity? I did! I mean, it does add value to your life because you want that degree, right? Small things like this make a HUGE impact on your success. Think about this the next time you are asked to do something you want to say "no" to. Mary Lebens, IT faculty at Anoka Technical College and Doctoral Candidate, suggested, "sometimes you just need to say no. That's the hardest part *is* prioritizing, and then dealing with those feelings of feeling guilty, or feeling like you're missing out. You'll get over it though, I promise. You can always use the fact that you're in school as your scapegoat for this as well *wink. *"

Take inventory

Taking inventory is similar to reviewing everything in your life. Completing this step lets you see where you are starting. In all honesty, here's where the real work begins. Ever heard the saying, "you have to know where you are now, before you can decide where you're going?" Here are few ways you can think about: you can think of it like a roadmap. In order to get from point A to point B, you have to have a point A. In terms of weight loss, before you can set your sights on where you want to be, you have got to know your starting weight, right? Well this is just like that. I must tell you now, this is going to get a little ugly (especially if you have a lot on your plate) however, I'm here to help you make some sense of it all.

The goal of this activity is to help you identify everything that you do... EVERYTHING!!! For starters, you are, or will soon be a college student or adult learner. Are you a parent? Take care of your elderly parents? Have a job? Engage in extra-curricular activities? Go to church? Go to the gym? The idea here is for you to list everything you do so that you can find a place for everything. At the same time, you can see if you need to let something go as well. This is a crucial part of the process so please, don't skip this step.

To start, get yourself the following items: blank sheet of paper, a pencil and whatever you currently use to jot down appointments (calendar, notebook, phone, etc.). I'm going to have you start with yesterday. Why? It already happened so it's easy for you to remember what you did. So, what did you do yesterday? Write these in list form on the blank sheet of paper. Now, do this again for the day before yesterday, and so forth. Essentially, you'll be doing this for the entire week. Was everything that you listed actually on your calendar? If so, perfect! If not, that's perfect too! This let's both of us know that you are in the right place! You should keep going through this process until you feel like you have captured everything that you do in a given week. Once you have completed this list, you are ready to move forward to the next step.

Action Item #5: Itemization of tasks

	What do you do? List each item here.
1	
2	
3	
4	
5	
6	
7	
8	
9	
10	
11	
12	
13	
14	
15	
16	
17	
18	
19	
20	
21	
22	
23	
24	

☐ **#alldone**

Prioritize

Now that you have your list in front of you, you can begin to categorize needs and wants. Simply put, needs are what you have to do, and wants, are what you'd like to do if you have the time. As a college student or adult learner, you should have a well-balanced life. I wholeheartedly believe that you can excel in school, work, hang out with your friends, be a great parent and all things in-between. However, you have to plan for this as much as you can. I can honestly say that when I was working on my doctorate, I went to weekly happy hours with my friends, socialized during weekly softball games, got my schoolwork done (completely and on-time), and ran a multi-million dollar behavioral health program, while also working as adjunct faculty for an online university. Not bragging, just telling you that it is possible.

People make time for what they believe is important, now it's your turn. Place a (W) next to the thing that fall under wants, and place a (N), next to items that fall under needs. As you go through this activity, be honest with yourself. I really want you to see how much you do. When we're done, I want to help you see that you can do it all, while you are earning your degree.

Action Item #6: Itemization of tasks

	What do you do? List each item here.
1	
2	
3	
4	
5	
6	
7	
8	
9	
10	
11	
12	
13	
14	
15	
16	
17	
18	
19	
20	
21	
22	
23	
24	

☐ **#alldone**

<u>Be still</u>

Well, you did it. You have a list of everything that you do. Now, I want you to walk away from it for the time being. Sit still. Sitting still allows you to reflect on the process that you are about to embark on. Check out some Oprah or Lisa Nichols on YouTube and spend some time reflecting. Try listening to Deepak Chopra and meditate. Listen to some of your favorite music. Hang out with friends. Whatever you do, just don't do anything related to organizing your life. You've done enough for now. You can mark this task off as #ALLDONE.

Chapter 5

People, Places and Things

5: People, Places and Things

Alex

Alex is the Love Engineer and Founder of **Dessert and Discussions (make sure ya'll check her out). All across the country, Alex hosts co-ed, fun-filled, thought provoking discussions about love and relationships. She also has a card game called, *the war on love.* Prior to stepping out and running with her passion, Alex was a mechanical engineer who held various roles of increasing responsibility in the supply chain at a large, well-known organization. Just like myself, Alex is known to frequent coffee shops in the area for inspiration and motivation.

One day after lunch, Alex and I went to a local bookstore/ coffee shop to get some work done. While we both worked on different tasks, simply being in each other's company, at a place that was conducive to productivity, served as the perfect atmosphere for us to become accountability partners. Over the span of a few weeks, we met a few times per week. She worked on her business: Dessert and Discussions, and I, either graded or worked on #ALLDONE. We would check in to see what the others' work tasks were for the day, chat a little and work a lot. It was a win-win situation: accountability and a partner to bounce ideas off of. I recall the day when Alex said she was able to make significant progress on her goals in just the short time we met up with one another.

Atmosphere

This entire chapter will focus on making sure that you have the right atmosphere to be successful. When I talk about atmosphere, I am talking about the classic 5W's and 1H that we learned about in school; who, what, where, when, why and how. Identifying your personal 5W's and 1H, will help you go so far.

When you find that you need inspiration or motivation, using everything that you list here will help get you back on track.

I like to take a proactive approach with this as much as possible. It took me a while to figure out my preferential atmospheres, however, once I got it, I got it (if that makes sense). There were times when I could not focus, did not have motivation and honestly, tasks would fall by the wayside. It happens to the best of us. However, if you want to be successful, you will want to have less non-productive days. When you can't motivate yourself, one, or a combination of a few of these items can help you get back on track.

Who

These are people that can get you on track or keep you on track. These are people that believe in you and will support you as you work to attain your goals. This can be a friend, family member, classmate, spouse, etc. Whenever I found myself lacking motivation, I knew that there were 3-4 people that I could always call to get me on track (or at least in front of the computer). This does not have to be someone who understands the work that you are trying to do, rather, a person that can give you some words of motivation and inspiration.

Sherry Wickstrom, Academic Dean at Anoka Technical College, shares a similar viewpoint about finding a supportive group of people. In our conversation, she stated, "it's something that I recommend for everyone no matter what stage of life they're in, and that is to create your own personal board of directors. Make sure that you have a board of directors. They will change as you encounter different things in your life. It's the people you trust, people that you know will give you a true answer...So in different times in life, you have different people who make that board of directors up."

Action item #7: When I need motivation and inspiration to stay the course, I can call one or more of the following people:

1. _____
2. _____
3. _____
4. _____
5. _____

What

I had a few conversations with others about knowing what you want. It's "your vision, your goal, set your goal and stick it," stated Shant'e Williams, Founder of Beaut'e Within. Jacqui Gilmore Stallworth, Creative Director & Founder of 10.30 Designs, had a similar view, when she stated "know what your vision is and write it down." Writing it down helps you keep your eyes on the prize, sounds cliché' but it's true. There's something about seeing your "what" written down that makes it more likely that you'll take the necessary steps to complete the goal.

Identifying what you are trying to accomplish keeps your sights set on success. Yes, you may have kids at home that you need to tend to. Yes, you might have deadlines at work. Yes, you are taking a few classes and you have many assignments to complete. I agree, this can all be VERY stressful, however, you must keep your eyes on the prize. Knowing what you want to accomplish can be your own personal motivation. When times get tough, think about what you are trying to accomplish. Sometimes, this is just enough to get you moving again.

Action item #8: What am I trying to accomplish? I want to:

1. _____
2. _____
3. _____

Where

Knowing the places where you can focus is crucial. Identifying where you can work effectively and efficiently is the premise behind identifying your "where." I learned early on that the library did not work for me. I also learned pretty quickly that trying to do schoolwork in bed only led to me taking an impromptu nap. I tried many things before I finally realized that getting out of the house was the best option for me. Places I tried were different common areas around campus, local bookstores, coffee shops, etc. Believe it or not, I wrote my entire dissertation between two places: a large bookstore chain and a common coffee shop. A few days a week, I'd go to one of these two places and get to work. Ironically, when writing papers, I could stay at home and work at my desk. I finally found my rhythm in terms of where I could write and actually get work done.

Now, your "where" might be different than mine, and that is ok. The goal is to identify what works for you. Have you ever noticed that you'd try to sit down and work on schoolwork, yet you can't focus because the place where you are is not conducive to getting work done? I'm sure that we are not the only two people in the world that this has happened to, therefore, I wanted to add this to the book.

Action item #9: When I need to focus on schoolwork, I can go to the following locations:

1. _____
2. _____
3. _____
4. _____
5. _____

When

This aspect refers to knowing when you are most productive throughout the day. Jeff Sanders, of the *5am miracle podcast,* calls this Identifying your FBOT or focused block of time. Identifying "when" will help you efficiently and effectively organize your time when you must get schoolwork and other tasks done. Are you an early riser? Do you function better at night? Do you write better immediately following the class? These are the questions that you should ask yourself because it will save you precious time when you sit down to organize your week. Once you identify when your ideal writing and studying times are, plan these into your schedule accordingly.

I recall the time I identified my "when." After I completed my work/school day, I tried feverishly to sit down and write a paper. I was so tired that I could not formulate thoughts or ideas. I was frustrated because I never recalled having this problem before. For a period of one week (could've been more), I tried to end my day with school work. In hindsight, I was doing so much (not bragging, more like doing too much), that when I finally sat down, all I wanted to do was sleep. This period of non-productivity left me behind in a few areas of my life. I became so stressed out, I had to ask one instructor for an extension. In one course, I decided to not complete an assignment because I was so overwhelmed. I knew that I could not operate like this too much longer.

I learned that I write my best during the following two times: immediately after waking up (for the day or from a nap), and when I changed my scenery. An example of this is leaving my bedroom to go to my home office or leaving the house to go to my favorite coffee shop. Now, it's your time to identify your when. Do you know when you have your best thoughts? Do you know when writing or working on school work seems to be effortless? As you complete your schedule later, keep these times in mind. These times can serve as a foundation for your day as you sit down and think about doing your school work. Take time to think.

Action item #10: The best times that I believe I can focus are:

1. _____
2. _____
3. _____

How

Kent Hanson, President of Anoka Technical College and Anoka-Ramsey Community College discussed why knowing how you plan your day is as important as knowing what you want to do. When he thought about his life while furthering his education, he talked about one of his main barriers: figuring out how to get everything done. A tip that he gave was to identify what you have to do and try to combine a few things if possible. Want to work out? Cool, try riding a stationary bike while reading for class.

Knowing how your day will be planned can ease stress and anxiety. As a busy student with a life outside of school, your day will most likely include a variety of tasks that you need to handle on any given day. You will endure a lot as a student, believe me, I know. However, preparing for this in a proactive way does make the day smoother. As you sit down and plan your day, you will notice that there are items that need to be put into your calendar or planner automatically. Do you have children in day care? Class? Work? Doctor's appointments? These items will be added to your schedule first and then you will plan other tasks around these.

Action item #11: The things that I must do during the week are the following:

1. _____

2. _____

3. _____

4. _____

5. _____

<u>Do you!</u>

Knowing yourself sets the stage for ultimate personal success. Using the steps listed above, you are better able to identify the key factors that work best for you. Yes, I'm sure that there are more factors that can be added in, however, I wanted to keep this as simple as possible so that you'll do the steps. Even if you find that your factors change over time, that's fine, work with it. The more you know about yourself, the better you will do when the time comes to start working through your assignments.

Chapter 6

School Tools

6: School Tools

Vignette

The moment you decide to step on (or log in) a college campus, you should already be thinking about how you will fit school into your daily life. As I think back on the times I started new academic programs, I sat with a variety of administrators, reviewed and signed a barrage of documents and stared blankly at materials that I felt were obsolete. During my current program, I realized how useful most of the information I received was (go figure). In this section, I will review some of the most common things you will get access to, as well as the ways you can use these items.

Registration

On college campuses, face to face or online, you can use items that you get access to because you are a college student or adult learner. Tools, lifehacks and opportunities for organization and task management can be found all around you. Let's start with the first thing you do when you sign up for classes: register.

When you go to register for classes, what do you think is the first thing you should be looking at? Aside from the actual course you will be taking, you need to make sure that you can attend the scheduled meeting times. For face to face classes, the schedule will be listed. You should plan to mark yourself as unavailable on your calendar for the timeframes listed. For online courses, if you have a synchronous component where you meet one time per week for lecture online, make sure that you block this time out in your calendar. For strictly online courses, you will need to organize your own time accordingly, however, you can begin to set aside when you will work on schoolwork. For those attending online, you will need to schedule everything on your own. If you are not organized, now is the time to start because it will only get more difficult as the course is actually happening.

The syllabus

Use your syllabus/instructor policies as a task management tool. Your syllabus dictates everything you must do throughout the course. As a student and instructor, I use the syllabus as my "holy book," my "place to go when I have questions," my "what the heck am I supposed to be doing now?" document. As a student, when I have a question: I go to the syllabus. As an instructor, when a student has a question: I point them to the syllabus! Feel free to use this to your advantage! At the start of the course and throughout the course: review the syllabus. Yes, I said it! REVIEW THE SYLLABUS! Here, you will find due dates, instructions, policies and your instructor's name *insert smile.* Seriously though, here's what I just did after I completed an assignment: looked at my syllabus, highlighted everything that I already completed in green, and highlighted everything that I still need to do in yellow. As I complete my tasks throughout the remainder of this course, I will turn that assignment green. There's something about changing the colors to green that makes it feel like a fun game to me. Use whatever colors you want, but try it out and see how it goes! Mark those assignments as #alldone!

Course schedule

The course schedule template is useful to help organize assignments, tests, readings etc. In using this template, you can see everything you need to complete for an entire course, all at once. This will help you conceptualize the amount of time that you will need to allot for schoolwork. You can complete one grid per course, or complete one grid, for multiple courses, my preference is one per course. Using the following rules, write in everything associated with one course that you are taking.

- ☐ Have a copy of your syllabus handy
- ☐ Based on due date, transpose the items from your syllabus on to the grid below
  *place any readings, videos and other supplemental materials onto the first day of the week

By the time you complete these items, you should have a fully completed course schedule grid for all of your tasks and assignments for one entire course. As you complete the items in the grid, put a line through the item so that you know that you completed it. As with the other items, this is a work in progress. If you feel that this grid works for you, use it for all of your courses, throughout the entirety of your program.

Action item #12: 8-week course template (copy twice for a 16-week course)

	M	T	W	TH	F	Sa	Su
1							
2							
3							
4							
5							
6							
7							
8							

Who's who on campus

Whether face to face or online, you will have a team of people whose sole purpose is to help you be successful. It would behoove you to make sure that you become very familiar with your team as early as possible. I like to call this the "in case of emergency" (ICE) list for your education. David Billingsley, Musician and Owner of BSOMA, talked about how important it is to use the things you get access to just for being a college student. He recommended that you take as many opportunities as you can to "network, do internships and visit your instructors during office hours. Take advantage of all that stuff, " as these items can only enhance your educational experience.

While your ICE list may be different from mine, here are a few folks that I found to be helpful during my academic journey:

Academic advisor. If you're anything like me, your academic advisor should be your best friend. I recall changing programs during my doctoral journey. My academic advisor was my sounding board for helping me navigate the process to make this seamless and smooth. He even helped me understand the differences between the programs so that I could make an informed decision prior to making the switch. I can only hope that you have a similar experience as I had with mine.

Department chair. The department chair is someone that you can turn to for questions about school processes. While I have never had to refer to the department chair, I have had some friends and students who did at one point in their college career. In the event that mediation is needed between yourself and an instructor, this person can serve as a mediator. Additionally, the department chair can also help link you with other people in your field. If you're thinking about networking, this is a great person to start with.

Instructors. As you go through your journey, you will want to get to know your instructors. Each instructor is different; therefore, you will need to learn how each instructor runs their courses. The biggest pet peeve of instructors is the line "my other professor didn't do things like this." Please don't say that to your instructor. It will not end well for you. Simply learn their way of doing things via reading their syllabus and/or instructor policies and viewing your rubrics and feedback when you get your grades back.

Financial aid office. If you receive financial aid to go to school, the financial aid office can be a great resource to ensure that you are aware of deadlines associated with financial aid. Additionally, this office is instrumental in ensuring that you have enough money to cover the courses that you plan to take. If you are nearing your max of loans, this office can ensure that you are aware of this as well. Make sure that you know who to contact in this office for your financial related needs.

Support services: Each college has its own version of support services. While it might not be called this specifically, identifying who your support services team is can be beneficial in the future. The people in this department help you succeed in your educational goals. Services such as counseling, clubs, disability assistance and tutoring services can be found here. If a time comes when you feel like you're getting behind, this is the place you can turn to before it's too late.

Campus groups

Campus groups are essential if you are looking to find like-minded individuals on campus or in your program of study. Whether you decide to use campus groups as a way to connect with other students on campus or to simply decompress, these groups can benefit you both on and off campus. Meeting people on campus can serve as a way to network with others. When you are done your college journey, these can turn into people that you will have long-lasting friendships with as well. Keep this in mind the next time you head on campus.

During my conversations with others about success strategies, many discussed networking on campus as one of the primary things a person should be thinking about while they're in school. Shameka Holloway, Senior Executive Training Manager of a large telecommunications company and owner of Classy Lady Boutique, is one of the people that discussed this specifically. In our conversation about the topic, she stated "don't miss the opportunity to connect with others on campus." Even if it's just a phone number or email, make sure you establish and maintain some type of connection. You never know when you'll need them or be able to help them with future endeavors, so don't take this lightly. Similarly, Harry Colbert, Managing Editor of Insight News, shared a similar sentiment. When you establish connections, "make sure they are genuine. When you build a genuine connection with someone, that resonates." A connection can turn into a job, which in fact, did happen to Harry, a few times over!

Classmates

Classmates can help you go a long way in your program. When you get stuck on an assignment, need an accountability partner or simply need to vent, your classmates can help you through the tough times. As an instructor and student, I have seen the benefit of students working together. Diverse approaches to completing/understanding assignments as well as student-centered ways of understanding assignments occurs best when students work together.

Getting to know other classmates can also help you identify small workgroup opportunities. If you happen to find someone that likes to schedule blocks of time to work on campus, at the library or in a coffee shop, this person can help you set aside some time to work on assignments uninterrupted. You will be lucky if this person also serves as a motivation and inspiration to get your schoolwork done as well.

Internship and volunteering

Internship and volunteering will set you up for success during your school journey and after. If you're going to school, I'm sure you're thinking ahead in terms of what you'd like to do for a career. While you are in school, you should be thinking about who you need to connect with and how you are going to connect with them. If you are lucky enough to have an opportunity to do an internship for your program, use this to your advantage. There seriously is no better way to learn about the field than being in the trenches, working in the field directly. If you must complete an internship, connect with people in the organization, really get your hands dirty and think of your brain as a sponge. Collect as much knowledge and experience as you can. The best thing about internships is if you do a good job, the organization might consider hiring you when you are done. This is the ULTIMATE bonus if you are so privileged to have this happen.

If you do not have an opportunity to intern anywhere, think about volunteering in your field of study. While I know that time is tight, try to squeeze some time in if you can. When you volunteer, you are still networking and learning about the field while being in the trenches with those that are doing that actual work. Use this to your advantage! Set aside some time to help others, this will also benefit you in the future.

Chapter 7

Grids, Templates and Other Tools

7: Grids, Templates and Other Tools

Vignette

Nina Keyes-Reid is a mother of 2. She is the owner and founder of Philly Cheesesteak Tours in Philadelphia, PA. Concurrently, Nina has been a school teacher in the school district of Philadelphia for 17 years. If that's not enough, Nina also models and is a real estate investor. In order to get everything done, Nina used a tried and true method to keep herself organized.

Nina's story is a story of success. Two weeks into undergrad, Nina had her son. After taking one week off, she went back to school to complete what she started. While in school full time, she worked and raised her son. In fact, she only ended up extending her planned 4-year school stint by one semester because she was unhappy with a grade she received, so she took the class again. When asked how she was able to get it all done, Nina stated "I wrote out everything and checked things off in the process." Nina is a firm believer in planning your schedule. In this chapter, we will discuss how you can be successful using a similar process.

Write it down

Ever have an appointment or something to do that you just knew you'd remember, only for the time to come and you forgot about it? Yup, me too. Just happened this morning! Truth moment; had it not been for writing the appointment down, I'd still be in my hotel room lounging and trying to capitalize on a late checkout. I pondered whether I was going to tell you guys and gals this, however, why not tell the truth? This LITERALLY just happened so I figured I'd share.

Writing things down helps you see exactly what you need to do on any given day. Additionally, it helps you get and stay focused whenever you feel like you're getting off track. In this chapter, I will discuss written forms of planners, calendar and grids. There has been extensive research on the effectiveness of using the standard pen and paper method, I'm just here to help you apply some techniques I've found helpful in real life. In this chapter, I will discuss different forms of written techniques you can use to be successful.

Bullet journal

Bullet journaling has been so helpful!!! If you could see me, I'm jumping up and down on my chair singing bullet journals' praises. I LOVE BULLET JOURNALING!!! Now, while I've always done lists to help get organized, I'd write my lists on random sheets of paper, napkins, or any other piece of paper that I could find whenever I decided that I needed to write something down. Problem is, I'd also easily lose this piece of paper as well. As I write, I'm chuckling because I have lost more important lists than I can count. It wasn't until I started using a bullet journal system that I realized having an actual book to document everything was the best way to keep everything together.

If you decide to do a bullet journal, it will become a way of life. I mean seriously, you won't be able to live without it. I put EVERYTHING in my bullet journal: doctor's appointments, meetings, other appointments, assignments, due dates, etc. Essentially, if I have to be somewhere or do something, it is in my bullet journal. My entire life is in this book, in an organized manner, so that I can purposefully organize my time in a way that allows me to get everything done. Now, bullet journals can be intricate or simple (mine is pretty simple), again, do what works for you. If you decide to go the written route, the bullet journal can be your best bet.

Daily list

The idea behind a daily list is that you can see what you need to accomplish on a given day. The good thing about the daily list is that you can lay your day out so you can see everything that must be done. Another good thing about this method is that you get a chance to see what can and cannot be done in a 24-hour period. When using this grid, hopefully you are allotting time to eat and sleep... I mention this because some people forget that they need to do these things... It isn't until they start laying everything out in front of them that people realize they might be trying to tackle too much.

When working on my daily layout, I am looking at a full week (7 days). The first thing I write in are assignment due dates. This helps me plan for how much time I need to spend on schoolwork in a particular week. Next, I add in when I teach face to face classes because this is an appointment, right? Then, I write in other appointments I have during this particular week if they are not already there. After that, I'm writing in grading time, because I have to do that as well. Client visits and other appointments get put in around that. Workout time goes in at the same time. Yes, yours will be different than mine, however, the premise is still the same. Enter what you must do first, then layer in what you want to do after that. The ultimate goal is for you to have time to do everything you set out to do.

Now, it's your turn. Below is a full, one-week template for you to try your hand at using a daily layout. The reason why I have 6 spaces is because it forces you to be realistic about how many tasks you can accomplish in one day. If you need more or less, feel free to add/take away, but please remember, the goal is to organize your life. Using the following rules, write down your schedule for the week in the order in which *they* appear.

- ☐ Write in assignment due dates
- ☐ Write in classes and other places you must physically be, etc
- ☐ Write in when you will work on assignments
- ☐ Write in other tasks (workout, shopping, etc)

By the time you complete these items, you should have a fully complete daily grid. As things come up throughout the week, add/change/amend your worksheet accordingly. Remember, this is a work in progress, try writing things in pencil until you get the hang of it. 9 times out of 10, you will forget something your first go 'round, so be patient and amend as needed.

Action item #13: Daily template

Monday Date:	1. 2. 3. 4. 5. 6.

Tuesday Date:	1. 2. 3. 4. 5. 6.

Wednesday Date:	1. 2. 3. 4. 5. 6.

Thursday Date:	1. 2. 3. 4. 5. 6.

Friday Date:	1. 2. 3. 4. 5. 6.

Saturday Date:	1. 2. 3. 4. 5. 6.

Sunday Date:	1. 2. 3. 4. 5. 6.

Weekly list

A weekly list helps you plan across the week. This view is great for goal-setting and pre-planning. I use the weekly list specifically for larger projects and tasks. Have an assignment due? You can use this to plan out the different steps across a few days. This also helps you avoid procrastinating and waiting until the last possible minute to complete assignments. Now, it's your turn, let's assume that you have an assignment due on Sunday. Using the following rules, write down your schedule for completing your assignment.

☐ Write the name of the assignment on the day of the week that it is due

☐ Break the assignment up into 3-4 manageable chunks, identifying what you will do on that specific day (example: research, outline, one section, etc; feel free to lay this out based on your own preferences)

By the time you complete these items, you should have a fully complete grid for completing your assignment. Again, this is a work in progress. Every time you complete this, you will notice that you get better at planning your assignments out. As you write this, you can also transpose this information into the daily list. Remember, your goal is to have this be livable, it has to work into your schedule, realistically.

Action item #14: Weekly template

M	T	W	TH	F	Sa	Su

Monthly spread

A monthly spread is useful for putting in appointments, deadlines, etc., in a monthly view so that you can see everything at a glance. At the start of each month, lay in a monthly view and write down what needs to be done on specific days. This can help you eliminate overlapping your schedule and keep you on track. Using the following rules, write down your appointments for the month. If you have a few things to do on any specific day, write in the time as well.

☐ Write in the days that you have class this month
☐ Write in assignment due dates for this month
☐ Write in appointments (doctor, dentist, kid's appointments, parties, other events)

By the time you complete these items, you should have a fully completed monthly grid for all of your appointments, assignments and places you must physically be. As with the other items, this is a work in progress. If this works for you, you will do this every month and add in items as they come up.

Action item #15: Monthly spread

April

1	Sa	
2	Su	
3	M	
4	T	
5	W	
6	Th	
7	F	
8	Sa	
9	Su	
10	M	
11	T	
12	W	
13	Th	
14	F	
15	Sa	
16	Su	
17	M	
18	T	
19	W	

20	Th	
21	F	
22	Sa	
23	Su	
24	M	
25	T	
26	W	
27	Th	
28	F	
29	Sa	
30	Su	

Pomodoro

The Pomodoro technique involves setting aside short periods of time to engage in a task. I like to use this method for those pesky little tasks that I keep putting off until the last possible minute. How this works is, for those tasks that you simply hate, give yourself a set period to work on it and be done. Whether it's cleaning, checking emails or that *pesky* assignment that will only take a few minutes to complete, the Pomodoro technique can be used. To use this technique, set a timer for 10, 15 or 20 minutes. During this time, you will work on the task. When the timer goes off, you stop. What I can personally say about this technique, is when you start the task and the timer goes off, you might not want to stop, but that's not a bad thing at all. Keep working until you get the job done.

Do nothing

There will be times when you just can't get yourself together. You're tired, can't focus, can't gather your thoughts, etc. When this happens, I will highly advise you to take time to simply do nothing. Sleep, rest, talk to a friend (not about all the tasks you need to finish), take a walk, enjoy the breeze; whatever will take your mind off of everything you need to do, do that! Sometimes a simple reset is all you need to be able to get reenergized. Now, I'm not telling you that you can do this every day, however, there will be times when you will need to do nothing. When it happens, don't feel bad. Use this as your time to reenergize and propel yourself forward.

Chapter 8

Plan for Success

8: Plan for Success

Vignette

Robert Farris is the Chairman and President of the CoNimby Foundation. Just like myself, he has 10+ years' experience as a college student. In my conversation with him, I was intrigued as he discussed his success story which involved growing up in group homes and being a "negative statistic" to becoming the Chairman and President of a lucrative foundation. The life from where he began to what he is accomplishing now appears to be barely recognizable, however, he used his upbringing as fuel for his success.

Robert, like many of the people I talked to as I wrote this book discussed success strategies that they felt I should share with you. You alone determine what success is to you. Your vision might be different from what others view as success, and that's ok. It's your life and your goal. When asked about tips he'd like to share with the reader of this book, Robert replied "create a career plan, create your path and follow through on it." While the road might have twists and turns, focus on your plan and path and use this as the framework for your ultimate success.

Review

In a conversation with Yataiva Harris, Industrial Engineer and Owner of HOM Group LLC, she discussed the importance of the review process. Now that you have everything in front of you, go ahead and look at everything that you have in front of you. When asked about the review process, she stated, "you're the main person that benefits from your own analysis. Take the time, sit down and think about what you need to do differently. After you have done that, adjust your plan accordingly."

You have reached the end of this book, and now, it's time for you to review everything that you have done. I took you through a few techniques and strategies, some of which may be new to you. As with any learning process, you might need to work through some kinks. Take the time to play with the different strategies that you see here. As you begin to feel comfortable with the technique, use it to the best of your ability.

Now that you have the steps, keep moving!

Erica Stene, Counselor at Anoka Technical College spoke about looking at your time in school as a means to an end in our conversation. Her viewpoint on the topic was "enjoy the process and understand that if I want this degree I also have to want to make this a part of my life in a way that it feels somewhat sustainable for this period of time and I can still enjoy life in the moment." School will not last forever. Make the best of your time there.

Now that you have the tools and strategies, it's up to you to decide what fits best into your current lifestyle. By now, you should have an idea of what works and what doesn't. Ask yourself questions such: as am I happy with this? Did I learn anything new? Is this applicable to my life and situation? Asking yourself these questions will help you process what happened and what needs to happen in the future. Amend and adapt accordingly. This is your program, designed by you, with your personal goal in mind: graduation.

Make it a lifestyle

Consistency is key when using the methods listed throughout this book. In conversations with many of the people I talked to while writing this book, being consistent might be one of the top tips I heard time and time again. Summer Willow Fitch, Proprietor, and William Fennell, Project Manager, both used a similar phrase when discussing things the reader should do to be successful. "Be consistent, as this is your means to an end," and "be consistent, practice it over and over again. When you make a decision to do something, you have to stick with it and commit to doing it!"

I am confident that whatever task management technique you use, it will become a way of life. Whether you decide to use a handwritten method like those discussed in this book or an electronic method, you will notice that your day won't go smoothly without having a list in place of things that you need to accomplish. I'll be honest, once I got into a rhythm, I use this system every day for schoolwork, work and life in general. Occasionally, I won't add items to my list. It is typically these times when I completely forget a task and them I am rushed to finish it... Don't do that! It's not a fun experience.

You can do this!

You can earn that degree and live life at the same time! Time will never stand still and we all have the same 24 hours per day to work with, therefore, we have to be as efficient as possible. Going back to why you are here, you need to learn how to effectively manage your tasks so that you can get everything done. Yes, you have to deal with things outside of school, however, using the techniques learned throughout this book, you can have fun and go to school at the same time. When you have a lot of things to do, this is easier said than done. There will be things that need to get done every day, similarly, there will be things that you will only need to do occasionally. Whichever your situation, you can learn to live your life while you earn your degree. Set yourself up for success ahead of ahead of time and plan to have a life at the same time.

Zakia Blain, founder and CEO of FBF Fitness talked about how planning your day will aid you in being successful. In our conversation, she stated you must "be a time-ninja! You have to schedule things down to the second and minute if you want to fit everything in... Make time for everything. Like it's a doctor's appointment, hair appointment, etc." Schedule things in your life in the same manner. You wouldn't cancel your appointment with your doctor or boss, don't cancel on yourself either.

Achievement

Day by day, assignment by assignment, course by course, you can achieve your goals! By reading and working through the activities in this book, you are already well on your way to achieving your goals. By having your tasks, events and appointments lined up in a uniform manner, you know what needs to be done and when, therefore, eliminating the possibility of forgetting what needs to be done. Jennifer Bingle, Principal and Owner of Strength Solutions, "it's hard work every day, but it's worth it."

As you make your way through your courses, go ahead and cross them off as complete. Before you know it, all of your courses will be complete and you will be walking across the stage at your graduation. How is that for achievement?!

Building blocks

Each step listed in this book can serve as a building block for your success. "There will be times in your life where you you'll think there ought to be a guide on how to get this done, and here it is!" stated Tien Sydnor-Campbell, Patient Governor for CreakyJoints. Similarly, Juneau Robbins, Owner of Cultural Chiropractic, stated by using this book, "you're empowering people to empower themselves, that's huge. When you give a person a vision of what they can potentially do, they tend to get up to their vision."

As you become comfortable with your technique, customize it, add to it, make it fancy, etc. I have seen some fancy bullet journal spreads that you might find work for you. Let Google, Pinterest, Facebook and the internet in general be your friend. If you want to jazz up the book that you will essentially carry with you everywhere you go, go ahead. There are groups you can find with like-minded folks around bullet journaling. I personally belong to groups that discuss bullet journaling as a general practice, but also some are more specific. The groups that I like the most are the groups for debt reduction, meal planning and school. The choice is yours to make.

Share your joys!

Finishing each course and ultimately completing your degree are joyous occasions! Terrell Brown, Founder of ImSoPhit, stated "you are well on your way to completing a lifetime goal that you have been working on since kindergarten. In using this book, you came across a tool to straighten up your college path, while others might have found through trial and error. Sharing your joy can excite your peers, family, admirers to follow in your footsteps to also achieve the same joy."

Now that you are done with this book and working towards your completing your degree, share your joys and success with others. By seeing that you are working towards and achieving your goals, you are inspiring others to do the same. Teach others some tips, share some insight, put your own spin on what you've learned, you will be surprised at how many people do not know how to effectively manage their tasks. Share your joys with me as well, I'd love to hear how you're doing. As you complete your courses, share your joys with me by tagging me in your social media post. As you walk across the stage to get your degree, tag me in that too! I'll be honored to cheer and share in your joys as you scream ALLDONE!

#ALLDONE!!!

Recommended by the Author